The INVENTION

of INFLUENCE

ALSO BY PETER COLE

The INVENTION

of INFLUENCE

Peter Cole

introduction by harold bloom

 A NEW DIRECTIONS BOOK

Grateful acknowledgment is due to the editors of the following magazines, where earlier versions of some of these poems were first published:

Almost Island (India): "A Palette," "Okay, Koufonissi," and excerpts from Parts One and Two of "The Invention of Influence"

The American Scholar: "Being Led," "Philo in His Confusion," "On Making and Being Made," "Six Cheers for Von Hofmannsthal," and from "The Invention of Influence": 'It's a mystical process'

Common Knowledge: "Actual Angels," "Abulafia Said That," "On Finishing," "The Reluctant Kabbalist's Sonnet," "On Coupling," "Summer Syntax," and from "The Invention of Influence": 'I don't know if you are right,' 'We held within us dark forces,' 'That a son can't bear his name'

Critical Quarterly (UK): "The Qualmist Aging"

Hambone: "On Being Partial," "What Makes Our Sense Make Sense," and "A Song of Dissent"

Island (Australia): from "The Invention of Influence": 'The great Talmudic sage Eliezer'

The Nation: "Leviticus Again," "Of Time and Intensity," and "Tutelary"

Paris Review: from "The Invention of Influence": 'Precisely this'

Poetry: "Song of the Shattering Vessels," "Quatrains for a Calling," and from "The Invention of Influence": 'Freud Could Never Be Certain'

Poetry Review (UK): "Summer Syntax" and "Notes from an Essay on the Uncanny"

Stonecutter: "The Perfect State" and "Self-Portrait in Pieces"

Triquarterly Review: "More for Santob"

The Yale Review: "What Is"

"On What Is Not Consumed" first appeared in *Sacred Trash: The Lost and Found World of the Cairo Geniza* (with Adina Hoffman, Schocken/Nextbook)

First published as a New Directions Paperbook (NDP1273) in 2014
Manufactured in the United States of America
New Directions Books are printed on acid-free paper.
Design by Eileen Baumgartner

Library of Congress Cataloging-in-Publication Data
Cole, Peter, 1957–
[Poems. Selections]
The invention of influence / Peter Cole; With an introduction by Harold Bloom.
pages cm
Includes bibliographical references.
ISBN 978-0-8112-2172-6 (acid-free paper)
I. Bloom, Harold. II. Title.
PS3553.O47325A6 2014
811'.54—dc23   2013039879

10 9 8 7 6 5 4 3 2 1

New Directions Books are published for James Laughlin
by New Directions Publishing Corporation
80 Eighth Avenue, New York 10011

ndbooks.com

For MRM—
Amazing friend,
inside the dream of the poem

CONTENTS

INTRODUCTION

I first came to know Peter Cole as a matchless translator of Hebrew poetry, particularly of the warrior Shmuel HaNagid and the skeptical mystic Solomon Ibn Gabirol. Those translations were gathered in *The Dream of the Poem*, a superb volume presenting the Hebrew poetry of Spain from 950–1492, and followed by his equally impressive *The Poetry of Kabbalah*.

Cole's original work achieved the strength of the translations with the publication of *Things on Which I've Stumbled* in 2008. His newest volume, *The Invention of Influence*, surpasses all previous Cole and confirms his standing as one of the most vital poets of his generation. In combination, the two books present a rare phenomenon in American poetry: maturation of individual stance and style through the prism of Hebrew and Arabic languages and literature.

With that transformation Cole has become one of the few American Jewish poets whose work is originally Jewish, a phrase in itself paradoxical. The only poet of my own generation who achieved an authentic Jewish voicing, John Hollander, had to overcome the early effect of Auden and a later agon with Stevens before he found a way to a Jewish idiom through his remarkable translation of Yiddish poetry: Moyshe-Leyb Halpern, Yankev Glatshteyn, H. Leivick, and others.

At times Cole's new poems remind me of elegant tonalities in Delmore Schwartz, a sad acquaintance of my youth, but Delmore worshipped (sometimes resentfully) at the shrine of T. S. Eliot, genteel anti-Semite and aggressive neo-Christian. And I suspect that only a high poetic decorum links Schwartz and Cole, who share the gift of almost never writing badly.

Peter Cole has become a writer in the Jewish wisdom tradition, building an open enclosure around a secularized scripture, which for him comprehends all of postexilic Jewish imaginative literature of the highest aesthetic and cognitive merit.

I turn to poems in *The Invention of Influence*, the long title poem in particular. Cole subtitles "The Invention of Influence" an "agon," in the spirit of Jacob Burckhardt and Friedrich Nietzsche, chronicling the Athenian struggles for the foremost place: in politics, thought, drama, victory odes, sports. But here the agon is the unequal contest between Sigmund Freud and his gifted disciple Victor Tausk, who killed himself after sending Freud a suicide note. Tausk, who was just forty, is remembered today as one of Lou Andreas-Salomé's lovers, part of a famous cavalcade including the poet Rainer Maria Rilke, perhaps Nietzsche, and, had age not shielded him, Freud himself. Tausk deserves a more positive memory than that.

Respecting Tausk, and finding in his struggle with tradition and his fathers a vulnerability reminiscent of the situation of the poet—of all poets—Cole in "The Invention of Influence" nevertheless avoids evoking remorse in portraying an overdetermined instance of character becoming fate. Intricately counterpointing the Tausk–Freud saga is the Jewish wisdom tradition, stemming from Tanakh and *Pirkei Avot* (*The Sayings of the Fathers*)—Hillel, Akiba, and the fierce Tarfon, whose ultimate saying both fortifies and admonishes: "It is not necessary for you to complete the work; neither are you free to desist from it."

Victor Tausk's self-defeat fails the test of Rabbi Tarfon, but Akiba, for all his greatness, was not Sigmund Freud and scarcely was accepted by Tarfon as a brother and not at all as a father.

Cole's version of Tausk's catastrophe sees the brilliant forty-year-old as a son unable to escape his awe of the heroic precursor, Father Freud, but unwilling to give in to it either. Cole's aesthetic and the ethos of Jewish wisdom fuse in a remarkably fresh balance of the joys and sorrows of the influence process. "Balance" is not quite the inevitable word: one would need the subtle dialectics of Moses Cordovero, the best speculative mind of Kabbalah, to encompass this venture of the *Heimlich* into the *Unheimlich*, Freud's Uncanny or remarkably Jewish Sublime. It is, though, just this combination that runs through this strange and powerful poem.

For in Cole's reseeing, one of the prime purposes of poetry is the formation and integration of a specifically Jewish self somehow centered upon translation, with that process reconceived in a sense both broad and cutting. Is this calling of an American Jewish poet (half of whose life is lived in Jerusalem on the Hebrew–Arabic divide) a new kind of aesthetic vocation? Our Father Freud fully expected to replace Judaism with psychoanalysis, and the man Moses by the man Solomon Freud. On one level, Cole wonders if the American Jewish poetic quest can evade some affinities with the audacious Freudian project.

Franz Kafka brooded that he might have created a New Kabbalah but for the burgeoning of Zionism, and Kafka is to Jewish literature what Dante is to Catholicism or John Milton to Protestantism: the archetype of the Writer. No matter that Kafka was equivocal about Judaism until his final relationship with Dora Dymant, when he returned to the study of Hebrew and dreamed of emigrating to Palestine with Dora.

Peter Cole's impulse in going to Zion was allied only in that he too sought a New Kabbalah. Myself a lifelong searcher for the Kabbalah of Harold Bloom, I have never found my sojourns in Israel useful for self-development, mostly because nobody in the Jewish state ever stops arguing or is silent enough to listen to anyone else. The Sublime exception was Gershom Scholem, too grand to argue, who greeted me genially as his "most surprising disciple" while saying of Kabbalah: "It's a free country." But then Scholem invariably spoke to me in the third person: "The opinion of so-and-so on this is such but Scholem always says" and the last word would follow. For me Scholem became Israel. Since he was a party of one, he represented only himself but that was more than enough. He taught me how to read Walt Whitman yet mystified me by affirming his trust in Yahweh.

Scholem also taught me the freedom of Kabbalah, a lesson reinforced by his great revisionist Moshe Idel. Peter Cole, though he never met Scholem, pursues that freedom in his poetry, which is profoundly informed by Kabbalah. Here is one of my favorites:

THE RELUCTANT KABBALIST'S SONNET

It is known that "desire" is, numerologically, . . . "the essence of speech."
Avraham Abulafia, "The Treasures of the Hidden Eden"

It's hard to explain   What was inside came
through what had been between, although it seems
that what had been within remained the same
Is that so hard to explain   It took some time
which was, in passing, made distinctly strange
As though the world without had been rearranged,
forcing us to change: what was beyond
suddenly lying within, and what had lain
deep inside—now . . . apparently gone
Words are seeds, like tastes on another's tongue
Which *doesn't* explain—how what's inside comes
through what is always in between, that seam
of being   For what's within, within remains,
as though it had slipped   across the lips of a dream

I would not have thought the sonnet could become a Kabbalistic form. Avraham Abulafia, court jester of Kabbalah, follows *gematria*, the mystical art of numerology, to declare "desire" the center of all speech acts. Cole, reluctantly yielding to overdetermination, finds himself besieged by what he has called "the mysteries of coupling and mediation, of the relation between surface and depth." But that is the dark heart of Cordoveran Kabbalah, where the *sefirot,* or ten primary modes of being, subdivide into six *behinot* or "aspects" each, one face turned toward or against another, a more-than-Freudian vision of the intricacy of psychic life.

The center of Peter Cole's exacting and often exhilarating poetic enterprise is the quest to transform seed-like words into "seams of being." A lyric variation, "Song of the Shattering Vessels," immediately precedes it:

> Now the lovers' mouths are open—
> maybe the miracle's about to start:
>> the world within us coming together
>> because all around us it's falling apart.
>
> Even as they speak, he wonders,
> even as the fear departs:
>> *Is* that the world coming together?
>> Can they keep it from falling apart?

The grandest of Kabbalistic tropes, Isaac Luria's *shevirat ha-kelim* (the Breaking of the Vessels), is refigured by Peter Cole as a lovers' kiss, or conversation. But that is what he wants from poetry, "reclamation and extension, connection and intense reconfiguration." That indeed also was the project of Lurianic Kabbalah, *tikkun,* or the mending both of the shattered kosmos and the wounded soul.

I recall writing somewhere, a long time ago, that prophetic Judaism (as I construe it) rejected *the injustice of outwardness* and called, with Jeremiah, for Torah to be inscribed within our inward parts. Cole, a strong poet, is kinder than that to outwardness, without which poetry becomes impossible. His marvelous hymn to outwardness, "What Is," closes this volume. The poem chants farewell to my friend of more than thirty years, the late scholar of Andalusia, María Rosa Menocal, who taught at Yale and died in 2012, at the age of fifty-nine.

"What Is" follows the downward path of the ten Kabbalistic *sefirot*: Crown, Wisdom, Understanding, Grace, Judgment, Splendor, Triumph, Majesty, Foundation, Kingdom. I read it closely because it is the crown of this volume and Cole's shrewdest adaptation of Kabbalah.

Perhaps Cole, only half-aware of her here, apprehends Emily Dickinson's presence throughout all ten of his irregularly rhymed quatrains. A journey is enacted in "What Is," the Death and the Lady courtship of "Because I Could Not Stop for Death."

The journey is María Rosa's away from the earthly paradise she only momentarily shared with her elegist. There is an intimation of Dante's Matilda gathering flowers at the highest reach of the *Purgatorio*, Canto XXVIII, but the starker shadow is Dickinson's poem no. 479, the likely source of Cole's "and children at recess dart into rings."

> We passed the School, where Children strove
> At Recess – in the Ring –

"What Is," Cole's poem-of-poems, also echoes Hart Crane's masterful "Repose of Rivers" from *White Buildings*. "A sarabande the wind mowed on the mead," Crane wrote, and that stately Andalusian dance appears in Cole as the *sefirah* Hod, Splendor or the Majesty of prophecy. Poetic fusion takes place here with a Kabbalistic verve, as it does in Dickinson and in Crane.

Standing back for perspective, "What Is" relies upon the *sefirot* not as difficult ornament but as composite trope for the loss of a beloved friend. And yet it is celebratory: its prime fiction is to enshrine "An instant's / happiness" in the company of the forever lost.

About forty years ago I composed a brief book called *Kabbalah and Criticism.* I recall saying that for me the *sefirot* are not images of the secret life of Yahweh. After all I do not like him, do not trust him and just want him to go away, but so strong a literary character will not.

The *sefirot* (I cannot speak for Cole, who has his mystical side) are for me a useful rhetoric, tropes constituting a truly critical response for the appreciation of poems. No active Kabbalist (we still have them) or scholar of Kabbalah would agree. Where are we to find the meaning of poems? My reply would be: "Wherever we can." Nietzsche perhaps thought that all metaphor commenced in the desire to be elsewhere, to be different. For me the *sefirot* are paths to elsewhere—no more, no less.

Cole, primarily a poet and translator, though one with transcendental yearnings, might agree but only in part. My angels are all like Enoch, undying men and women, yet undying only in Walt Whitman's sense: they will live on so long as they go on being remembered. Peter Cole's angels, like Benjamin's and Kafka's, are figures for everything our impatience has forgotten:

> Are angels evasions of actuality?
> Bright denials of our mortality?
> Or more like letters linking words
> to worlds these heralds help us see?

Going on eighty-three I am wary of prophecies. Nothing is final. Cole may presage a new kind of American Jewish poet or he may prove a party of one. This is a book to which I will often return in my remaining years.

Harold Bloom

… that these aural perceptions really exist
and are in some manner transferred
to my central nerves, and like in a telegraph
receiving station, are brought to my
consciousness, even perhaps not through the
ears alone, but …

Hugo Rennert
My Present Condition

I

OF TIME AND INTENSITY

Is Time a dispersion of intensity?
For epiphanists, maybe, but not for me—
for whom Time is a transposition
of immensity into a lower key.

ON BEING PARTIAL

I'm partial to what's possible,
he thought—not the ineffable,
distant, devoid of insistence
and temperament that tampers,
or tramples
            Not the impersonal,
but that which hovers here
between the "I" of the opening
and the "us" of your possible listening
now, or in the imperfect
tense and tension of what
in fact articulates the eternal
That abstract revelation
and slippery duration
to which, it seems, I'm given
and because of which I'm never
finished with anything, as though living
itself were an endless translation

ACTUAL ANGELS

"And Jacob sent messengers";
Rashi stated, actual angels.

I.

Are angels evasions of actuality?
Bright denials of our mortality?
Or more like letters linking words
to worlds these heralds help us see?

2.

It's the freighted angels that elevate.
Opaque with their burdens, they wait

for someone to sense what's there, between,
until they're released to the weather again.

3.

Gone is the griffin, the phoenix, the faun.
Only angels in the poem live on

as characters catching the light between things,
as carriers of currents from the wings

of thinking we know where we're going and then
getting somewhere, despite our intention.

4.
Maybe an angel's confused with an angle
so often because the slip lays bare
something these envoys are trying to tell us—
that what we're missing is already there.

5.
The light off of the Sound this morning
is like the sound of the morning's light—
a high-pitched, crisp, silvery ping,
though not of burnished wings, touching.

6.
Angels also act like classics,
tilting us toward the oddly real—
as with the crust of their reputation,
they block off access to it as well.

7.
How is it that creatures with names like Anáfiel,
Shakdehúziah, Azbúgah, and Yófi'el
could possess the power to raise a person
up to a Temple-within from his Hell?

8.
Angels are letters, says Abulafia,
in us like mind as the present's hum.
No one knows what a year will bring,
but the world-to-come is the *word* to come.

9.
He faces the Eden history is sweeping
him out of with a wind so relentless
eternity's storm pins back the wings
he's raising to break his curious progress.

The future to which he's backing in
brightens the rubble of what might have been.

10.
Messenger RNA is ephemeral—
like an angel, dispersed through a cell.

After translating coded instructions
that activate certain somatic functions,

it passes like prayer out of existence,
thus ensuring its own persistence.

11.
Borges likens his Aleph to Ezekiel's
four-faced cherubs facing at once
every direction—something conceivable
as well in the circuits of a quatrain's hunch.

12.
The elm slides liquid leaves through its sleeves—
its twig-tips swell with a ruby-like glow;
seraphs of jade then crown this mage,
their wings spreading the shade we know.

13.
Then the angels appeared to appear
within the skeptic's suspicion of what
hovered beyond the sight or thought
he'd hoped would make his position clear.

But there he was, suddenly estranged
from who he assumed he'd always be—
that gap drawing him into an obliquity
of being those legates had just rearranged.

14.
Angels anchor, like poles to being,
stretching the tent of a self's vision
beyond what it, doubtlessly, would have been
without that dent-and-inflection from heaven.

15.
An angel-like body about our bones
binds us to the luminous form
of the King-on-High's Presence below—
its skin the secret spelling of his name.

Thus a Kabbalist, in the fourteenth century,
weirdly as though he were speaking to me.

16.
We're getting closer to understanding
how angels slip inspiration by us:
science shows its wing-like spikes in
the superior interior temporal gyrus.

17.

It's an endless battle for the angel, said the scroll—
now against coarseness, then against light:
and radiance lines a mind's darkness,
as baseness defines a kind of height.

18.

Enoch ascended to heaven and saw
seraphs posted at fiery stations,
encircling I-AM's Palace of Awe.
All this—by means of translation.

19.

What the day is spelling out
recalls, in its way, revealed scripture
concealing the real, as the Psalmist says:
He turns the wind into his messenger.

ON FINISHING

The sober Saba isn't diminished
by noting his poems are never finished

ON COUPLING

Lacking the finish and fullness they crave
they follow a path that the couplet paves

o

The aim is a presence that's off in the distance
but there in the syllables' secret persistence

o

Strangely insistent, the syllables rely
on valencies greater than any one I

o

Or they might have known . . . let's call it a genius
for turning what's disparate into an "us"

o

Not just the moment's *feast-that-won't-last*—
the pleasures there in a present past

o

And, a future somehow forecast—
words like sails unfurled from a mast

o

Of talk that doesn't come to a close,
of somehow knowing the other knows

o

With calculation bodies descend
into desire—for what won't end

o

In giving the pleasure that makes souls bend,
they try to ward off an end they intend

o

Drifting together toward the ether
of passion that belongs to neither

o

Again they're descending, but now it's a fight;
he's read Heraclitus: opposing unites

o

A thousand things clattering; then a sign—
that singular thing—as though by design

o

Since character's fate. And that's what they are:
two become one that has taken them far

o

Into this symmetry, which is closer to life
than sprawl that's organically numb to strife

o

So it is that a coupling's rhyme
threads us, sometimes, through the sublime

A PALETTE

Azure lobelia props up the heart
 that extra hair's breadth happiness is.

———

The brown-hooded sparrow alights on a sprig
 which bounces, as though on the soul's trampoline.

———

Chicory blue diffused like sky.
 The Romans thought it barbaric.

———

Death's soot at the cypress's top—
 where the crow slows, and builds its nest.

———

The eye's dome inside the locust:
 the lime-green golden glow ascends.

———

Finches inch their way up a branch,
 blushing at being so subtle?

———

Gray ashes, containing lashes,
    in a tin can is his father.

———

Honest work makes itself known,
    somehow. This too is a hue.

———

Iodine is evening's aching
    for an elusive perfection.

———

Jasmine wafting. That sweetest shade of heaven
    on earth, August 8th, 2011.

———

Khaki seeks to keep the peace
    as a kind of camouflage.

———

Lavender leaves are *not* lavender.
    And then the spike of its pistil climbs.

———

Minium isn't mahogany;
    majolica blue is not maroon.

———

Nothing occurs in the way of color
for N. Is there a color of Nothing?

———

O, oleander, how many years
have I been writing this pure white poem?

———

Pelargonium's flesh-white sex
streaked with pink in the soft dawn light.

———

A quince stinks much less than guava
and keeps the alphabet alive.

———

Rust reduces iron to dust;
over time instead trust litheness.

———

Sepia tilts the actual into
the light of a slightly milder notion.

———

Truth is clear, as tea: visible only
there in the tincture that looking bequeaths.

———

Umber always hovers under
    the red of whatever gets said.

———

Verdigris takes on a value
    that's only understood with time.

———

Wheat rekindles the spectrum of . . . what? Wheat.
    Imbibing light from every direction.

———

X is always Albers's variable
    dynamic of ambient pigmentation.

———

Yellow stresses the Jew's encounter
    with what the world has put on his plate.

———

Zaffer's not saffron—it's cobalt,
    circling back to the azure start.

MORE FOR SANTOB

(de Carrión, 14th-c. Castile)

1. EVERYONE'S SO HIGH

Everyone's so high on "Yes."
Nothing has made me happier, though,
than the day I asked my lover if
she had "another"—and she said "No."

2. SPELL IN PRAISE

A choir of quatrains
    in praise of the servant
who asks of me nothing
    for what he does.

For years he's afforded me
    spectacular favors,
as though in fact he
    served out of love.

He somehow bears—
    though slight in stature—
the weight of the world
    within his words,

and blind he sees
    what I hold in mind;
deaf he absorbs
    what I've not yet heard.

He knows what I want
    before I've spoken,
and without speaking
    says who I am.

And so I've done
    as my debts demanded,
and sung for this spell
    in praise of the pen.

3. HOW FRIENDS ACT

Is anything better
than a pair of scissors,
which separates those
    that separate them?

They do this not
because they're bitter,
but out of desire
    to meet again.

When they're joined,
they do no harm—
hand to hand
    and lip to lip;

only when parted
can they destroy—
that's how strong
    their loyalty is.

Those who'd learn
what brotherhood means,
and how friends act
    when all is done,

should watch as scissors
make one of two—
and when they have to—
    two of one.

4. FOR BEING BORN

For being born
on a bush of thorns
the rose is certainly
    worth no less—

nor should wine
be scorned that's fine
but comes from lesser
    parts of the vine.

The hawk is likewise
no less blessed
because it was born
    in a humble nest—

and proverbs aren't
less noble or true
for being spoken
    by a Jew.

PARANOIA: A PROLOGUE

The life of man whose heart is a fort
is solitary, brutish, nasty, and short.

And the price at which that man can be bought
is what he's worth—is what Hobbes taught.

Felicity, he wrote—and maybe bliss—
is desire's perpetual progress

from one object on to the next.
The mere possibility of rest

is taken off the logical table,
and the only peace we're capable

of knowing, in *this* life, is Power's
(not eternity's in an hour)—

Power, that is, over desire
for Power. And so, we conspire

in fiction's lie against uncertainty
as though in a union under Divinity—

submitting before the King of the Proud,
like Job submitting at last before God.

A Great Wall against Suspicion
is built by the people, in their ambition,

who desperately want to avoid the war
that lurks beneath civility's floor.

"Where in this," you ask, "is the vulnerable?
Could anything be more abominable?"

But he understood: It's all about vain-
glory, or gain—we pay with pain—

and the middle way of a keeled humility
depends on cognition of a common fragility—

which is to say, a vital modesty
that's far more elusive than we can see.

Hence his lines, as the end came near:
"My mother bore twins—me and Fear."

PARANOIA: A PRIMER

1.
The paranoid parses all she hears
until it sounds like what she fears;

she fears what's always about to be said,
and so her fear is endlessly fed.

2.
Around her head like a halo it hovers,
a nimbus of hatred of self that smothers

others as well in the smog of its knowing
that knowing is never what's really going

on, and so on, and on it goes—
further and further from what love does.

3.
She ponders the sea of poisonous thoughts
that teach not a thing but *can* be taught.

Within the whirlpool of her mind,
she's caught as Life is left behind—

like a swimmer, swept out to sea on a tide,
which holds that nothing she's had to hide.

4.
A loom loud through the warp of her soul,
set in a room, beyond her control

and behind what anyone said, everywhere—
such were the fruits of her despair:

the choreography of her defense
against the contraptions of Influence,

the strings pulled, as though from afar,
jerking the puppets that we are.

SONG OF THE SHATTERING VESSELS

Either the world is coming together
or else the world is falling apart—
    here—now—along these letters,
    against the walls of every heart.

Today, tomorrow, within its weather,
the end or beginning's about to start—
    the world impossibly coming together
    or very possibly falling apart.

Now the lovers' mouths are open—
maybe the miracle's about to start:
    the world within us coming together
    because all around us it's falling apart.

Even as they speak, he wonders,
even as the fear departs:
    Is that the world coming together?
    Can they keep it from falling apart?

The image, gradually, is growing sharper;
now the sound is like a dart:
    It seemed their world was coming together,
    but in fact it was falling apart.

That's the nightmare, that's the terror,
that's the Isaac of this art—
    which sees that the world might come together
    if only we're willing to take it apart.

The dream, the lure, isn't an answer
that might be plotted along some chart—
    as we know the world that's coming together
    within our knowing's falling apart.

THE RELUCTANT KABBALIST'S SONNET

It is known that "desire" is, numerologically, . . . "the essence of speech."
Avraham Abulafia, "The Treasures of the Hidden Eden"

It's hard to explain   What was inside came
through what had been between, although it seems
that what had been within remained the same
Is that so hard to explain   It took some time
which was, in passing, made distinctly strange
As though the world without had been rearranged,
forcing us to change: what was beyond
suddenly lying within, and what had lain
deep inside—now . . . apparently gone
Words are seeds, like tastes on another's tongue
Which *doesn't* explain—how what's inside comes
through what is always in between, that seam
of being   For what's within, within remains,
as though it had slipped   across the lips of a dream

II

THE INVENTION OF INFLUENCE: AN AGON

PART ONE

The following considerations are based upon
a single example of the "influencing machine"
complained of by a certain type of schizophrenic patient.
                    Victor Tausk (Vienna, 1919)

It's a machine, said the doctor,
    of a mystical nature—
reported on at times by patients.
    Their knowledge notwithstanding,
witnesses are able to offer
    only the vaguest of hints
as to how the air loom functions.
    It makes them see pictures. It produces
thoughts and feelings, and also removes them,
    by means of mysterious forces.
It brings about changes within the body—
    sensation and even emission,
a palpable kind of impregnation,
    as one becomes a host.
For some it's driven by faint effluvia
    derived from human breath;
for others electric charges are sent
    directly into the brain.
It's born of a need to explain the cause
    of things inherent in man.
Certain factors are always involved:
    Enemies. Displaced erotic

tension. Boundaries are called into question
    as though one's thoughts were "given"
and knowledge implanted from beyond—
    so what's within is known.
One does nothing on one's own.
    Strings are pulled and buttons
pressed, all to evade an anxiety
    that rears its head at the heart
of the void in avoidance. The echoes begin:
    The cure as illness, the illness
as cure. Thus the revolving door
    that becomes a lament for the makers—
and for those who fall prey to the powers—
    of this most intricate machine.

———

    "By three things
        the world is hung"

—is strung among the Fathers' Sayings

(absorbing them we become like sons).

So this is among the sayings of the sons—

    Without these things
        the world's expunged:

        instruction is one,
            devotion another,
    and the constant bestowal of kindness

is the third
thread said the father who'd serve
in the warp and weft of daughters and sons

———

That I am a son, said Tausk,
   around the time he encountered Freud,
      causes me great embarrassment
(it shames me)
when someone calls me by the name
      handed on by my father ...

because a father conceived me
and a mother brought me into this world.
Destiny's what the eyes can see,
the ears take in, the hands contain—
still we're called to account with the elders,
and blood misled, misleads again.

And so with a needle he pierced

that picture's heart—
his mother

on the wall

———

No one will tell you, they said, about Tausk ...

Victor Tausk—

2.
It always begins
with simple sensations
        of change within
harmless at first,
then coupled with
a sense of estrangement

without awareness
of a source
        in control
and then with one
within oneself
but not oneself

In the case of Miss N. it appeared
to be wholly beyond her,

somehow like
a silk-lined coffin
    containing another,
but with a head that might be hers—

as though the dead were speaking,

or something dormant in her

————

What is instruction? asked one son.

Instruction is knowing—

not just what it *means* to be One,
but how to know how that needs to be done.

And what is devotion, wondered another.
Devotion is slaughter, a rabbi answered,
    of self in prayer like a fledgling dove,
    of self in the service of what we love.

And kindness?

Kindness said one
from the town of my fathers—

Kindness links worlds—below and above.

———

Miss N.'s invention was wholly hostile;
but at the heart of the art it involved,
it would be fair, said Tausk, to equate
the machinations of love and hate.

———

I must
       dig out
            my better self—
give up on my position and plunge
           into uncertainty
      before it's too late
    he wrote

at the dark gate to the soul
you—your own son now,
horror your guest,
　　　as the wounds widen …

Do what it is you've come for
Rend and render yourself without pity

For a grand god has called you

All the hours are gathered quietly
into the secret chamber—
　　and the spirit stumbles over itself
　　about the grave of your family

3.
"He saw a skull floating by on the water"

(water bearing the fathers and sons):

Hillel the Elder (father unknown)——

You drowned others and so were drowned,
and those who drowned you in time will be drowned.

The skull is Pharaoh's, said one of the sons
of the sons, and who,
                    said another, drowned him?

                    o

A third rabbi demurred:
the skull floating by was a friend——

and one of the sons of the sons of the sons
thought of the father's saying:

          "Know where it is you come from
          And where it is that you're going
          And before whom you will stand"

          ———

but everyone knows
what I'm thinking,
     or what I've discovered
          they've long known

because they set it
out for me,
    because it was set
        out for *me*—

the language we speak—
the language we seek—
is the language spoken
our words emerge
from beyond
(within)

our innermost thoughts are foreign,
implanted with great cunning

Thus the outer
    world of the inner
world that all can see

and that inner world of what's beyond me—

it shames me

———

"Among the sacrifices . . .
        we must count
Dr. Victor Tausk," wrote Freud

"This rarely gifted man

a Vienna specialist in nervous diseases

who took his life
before peace was signed."

4.
I have no right
      to act as I do,
            it isn't my business
                  to seek new paths,
but to provide for my children.

"Tausk is a man like any,"
said a friend, "who has to do his duty."

How deeply his words have touched me.

Touched me as catastrophe.

Why shouldn't I
      try—I
haven't really tried
anything
         in my life—

he wrote his wife
         at twenty-six,

      a father of sons
         (1906).

Instead I've been pressed
into a mold.

——

What would be is calling
    with voices like those
of shy children,
    a barely conceived
will to survive,
    to live, to thrive
faint through the din
of the clanging day.
These are inklings,
    kin to what
one might become.
And yet, the waves
    at times close in,
and what is shy
    begins to die;
one sees it there
in eyes
    greeting others
as though they were searching
for brothers....

—————

Said one of the sons of one of the fathers,
    in the name of Eliezer, and others:

Set your brother's honor as yours—
    within your name, feel his shame;
and be not easily angered—
    anger coils in the hearts of fools;
The day before you die repent—
    which always might mean now;

Warm your blood by the sages' fire—
    the tongues of which light worlds before you;
Beware, though, of their glowing embers—
    lest you be burned by wanting to know;
for their bite is the bite of the fox—
    whose tricks will rip through flesh;
and their sting is that of a scorpion—
    with pain so keen it sings;
and their hiss is the hiss of the serpent—
    the saintly, too, have their venom;
and all their words are fiery coals—
    with flames that, flickering, lick and maim.

———

"Lonely," he wrote on his own from Berlin,

explaining how he despised the dependent
because they made him
    dependent in turn
    and forced him to take his revenge
    and set himself free once again—
        as guilt accrued,
    and self-contempt—

"I can't communicate
with a soul,
my heart is so tired"
        (but knows)

wide worlds without words
are weaving

deeply in me hidden powers ...

———

"not a slave, because
not a master ..."

5.
Ahrweiler on the Rhine, 29 September 1907
a letter:
    "Salvation . . . a way of life
in which the heart gets richer
because you can daily practice the rites
of love towards genuine people."

Or earlier—

    "What would help me is money,
pleasure, success . . . the heart is anxious,
the lung has a catarrh. I need
to clear my head, control my nerves."

30 September, to Martha-in-Vienna (estranged):

"The whole of my past appears to be nothing
but preoccupation with this collapse.
If I have never believed in the power
of blood—now I believe . . ."

———

                    Later:

"By evening a true neurasthenic's thinking
grows clearer. . . . I took a wonderful walk
into the night . . . beautiful air. . . .
The doctors alone have intelligent faces.

The patients look like poisoned rats.
I'm not getting any treatment at all.
My lung is improving. For six weeks
I have been coughing, in competition

with my sons. I shouldn't write
such long letters—the doctor told me ...
to be lazy. . . ."

o

11 October:
"Getting better ...
      now it remains
to be seen."

———

And what you received, he wrote, *from your kin,*
      in time will come down to your sons ...
and the whole of your furious life will turn
      out to be but a day before dying.

6.

As one on high he's chosen calls—
the voice of a father summoned
through his blood as ink, spilt,
splits within his thinking's reach:

The Will will always roll out words
groping its way ... Between limits,
between limits the doubt dies—
your blindness, the wall before your eyes,

and yet you know the pain of the dark
light that is life with all its sorrow,
where people live ... See with me,
through this lens ... the limits extend.

Thus the banished ghost on high.
And he below the sublime one replies:

"Your word soars in a world
where I can't follow with my sorrow
Free my wings ... take my words—
all that remains of my action now.

The more I see, the more it burdens me.
How am I supposed to be—
to bear, refuse, endure, and give
or give in. And yet, I live

keeping step with the shadow of things,
alive, but only in the mirror
of living's skin. I can't bear
the thought that far away a day

and love exist, and blessed being."
Again his exalted rabbi rebukes him:

You're using far too short a measure,
the standards you hold to make you err—
you crawl along, weary of questions—
your "doing" is nothing but a way to wait,

and so the world, which should be home
(a house crowned with a noble death),
is pressed by death within the life
you move through as a shadow moves

under a rock about to fall....
And you've become your suffering and sorrow.
"You humble me even more than the world;
for all you've said means I have lived

a lie," he swallowed, which somehow echoed:
Who are you to hate yourself so?

"I know what I've been; hence my contempt
when I'm aware of myself beneath me.
But what am I supposed to be?
What? What might I be made of?"

Redemption attends to How, not What,
observed the one (within him) above.

7.

April 1908, he writes:

We muster a tentative Yes to our life,
unsure of just how much we can give.
Little by little we master our doubts
and begin addressing ourselves as a friend.
Gently fill the bowl to the brim,
or rather, let the bowl fill.
The task is to carry it, full, uphill.

———

There's a strange step
behind the door—
It fills me.
I hear it all.

I feel the coldness of the wall.
The handle turns ...
And between the door and jamb,
a strange face—like mine ...

Vienna, 18 February 1909

8.
Let the dead be.
Let them rest.

The dead won't ever
have to race
or shuffle through filth
and shame again,

or seek to suck
salvation from heaven.
The dead don't ever
have to listen.

This isn't religion.

The dead won't wake
with a morning's fright—
no ancestors come
to rebuke them at dusk.

Let them rest.

But if it turns out
that you're derived
from the dead
whose messengers arrive—

if you're driven—
don't render your life
more difficult still
(or your dying).

If you've been chosen,
don't resist.
Let them be.
It's good to rest

and see what they see.
Let the dead be.

PART TWO

Now what is going to happen
only Freud and God know. . . .

Tausk, Summer 1909

Invention isn't god-like:
    it doesn't create out of nothing.
It works through what's found: it discovers,
    and much like influence, it recovers

a charge that's already there,
    potentially, in the air.
All bodies are capable
    of being (mechanically) thrown

into a state in which
    they're said to be *electrified*.
Francis Hauksbee, the Elder,
    England, 1706,

constructed what's now known
    as an Influence Machine.
A crank turned a spindle,
    which rubbed insulated matter

against a spinning globe
    of glass—an emptied vessel
really a vacuum chamber—
    filled with mercury vapor.

The friction caused a shift
    and transfer of such force
along a conducting body—
    it took on a luminous glow

inside that bordered void.
    The glow of life, some called it,
shimmering like a TV.
    And so power could be

sent through a person's hand
    or room, and then across
the spinning globe, giving
    light to a body by it.

In these Orbs of matter,
    Hauksbee observed, *we have*
some little Resemblance of the Grand
    Phaenomena of the Universe …

What looks like nothing—holds everything,
    including a warning to all
would-be inventors: Remember—
    machines of this sort aren't toys,

and they're dangerous when mishandled.
    A basic contraption comprising
a charged pint-sized capacitor
    can incapacitate, or kill.

2.

From minutes taken
    on 18 May 1910
(Wednesday evening),
the Vienna College of Physicians:

The fraying feeling
    arises like this:
when one love dies
    and another exists

or is simply
    (the comment is Stekel's)
about to be,
the I unravels

or starts to dissolve,
    said the physician,
(whose Wednesday patients
    were often fictions—

his flair is for,
    said Freud, the hidden)
and ego-feeling
    alters, for certain.

Gaps are opened
    within the real,
which echoes like doubt—
    or debts we feel

and may have forgotten,
    returning as

the weird condition
      we'll call tradition.

Freud concurred;
      then added that we
see this with words
      we're used to using

suddenly seeming
      strangely strange.
Tausk said this
      can be explained

by the loss of affect
      words maintain
within the sentence
      (psychic syntax).

Experience (he
      suspects) suggests
the sense of estrangement
      at root is mixed

with guilt. Perhaps
      that feeling of strangeness,
he bizarrely
      deduces, tells us

nothing but this:
      if I see what I am,
my life must end
      by my own hand.

———

Talk about strange—in a haunted way:
   Tausk recently told me,
reported Lou Andreas-Salomé,
   how after times of strong

intellectual productivity
   which had been ended forcibly
by a distraction from without,
   though possibly from within,

he would become acutely aware
   of certain lines and forms.
He could stare at the leg of a table,
   an S-shaped ornament's curve,

as though that swerve suggested a whole
   world of inner relations—
as though he'd observed, at one and the same
   time, all that had gone

into bringing them into being
and found there boundless joy and fulfillment.

———

Knowledge was instinct—for survival,
and so he would stress the ego's defense
against anxiety, and flee intense
inspection of the self as rival—

drawn to its depths through the oblique
experience of a surface he'd seek.

3.

After, Lou recalled,
  Tausk's lecture
on the Father Problem,
  Freud was waiting
for me in the street. He
  was restless—Tausk's
ideas were close to his,
  and during the talk
he'd passed me a note, asking:
  "Does he know
all about it, already?"

——

He left an uncanny impression, said Freud,
who felt the disciple somehow in him—
thinking his thoughts though out ahead of him,
under his skin. Whose ideas
were *his*? What sort of sympathy *was* this?
Something deeply familiar, but strange,
which rendered one oddly at home in the foreign
and also alien to what one had been.
Where would it take them? What could be known
on one's own? Weird is the word
that suited him—as in what was destined.

——

Precisely this
  afflicts the plagiarist,

or something like
    the X he is:
What's old and has
    long been known
seems to him new
    and becomes his own.
He's all reception,
    all alone,
and the fruits are manifold
    though the root is one—
thwarted ambition
    and a sense at heart
the doctor describes
    as a kind of cry:
I cannot bear
    not to have been
the first to have uttered
    a certain thing.

———

Freud said he could never be certain,
in view of his wide and early reading,
whether what seemed like a new creation
might not be the work instead
of hidden channels of memory leading
back to the notions of others absorbed,
coming now anew into form
he'd almost known within him was growing.
He called it (the ghost of a) cryptomnesia.
So we own and owe what we know.

Invited to Freud's Friday evening.
      Talked at length of the Tausk problem.
Home at two thirty in the morning.

———

"From the first stirrings of the dream," wrote Lou,
"through to the place where we're fully conscious,
            we are only en route."
And this too—
      "Poetry is something between the dream
            and the reading."

Which might be just: Poetry is something between . . .

———

To be a link
to something more

and in that thinking—
to know its core.

4.

The great Talmudic sage Eliezer,
before he became a rabbi and master
and said all he said he'd heard from his teacher,
was hungry and wanted to learn. He was twenty-
two years old, the son of a farmer
he told he was leaving the land to study
in the city, though he wasn't ready.
His father forbade him from tasting food,
and leaving, until he had finished plowing
a long furrow filled with stones.
Then he was gone. Such was his hunger—
he still hadn't eaten—that while he was walking
he picked up a stone to put in his mouth.
He'd eaten dirt all his life.
Eliezer was hungry. The son of a farmer
unfed by his father's furrows and future.
He reached an inn and spent the night.
At dawn he went to Ben Zakkai,
famous already as Wisdom's father,
and sat at his feet, there in the dust.
A stench wafted up with his breath.
"How long has it been, my son, since you've eaten?"
Silence. He asked him again; and again
nothing. And Ben Zakkai taught him:
"Only when hunger becomes insufferable
not just to oneself, but to others,
will it bear fruit it doesn't devour.
As the odor is rising from your mouth,
so your fame for learning will travel."
And he would confess, a lifetime later—
"A single dog can lick from the sea
more than I've managed to take from my teachers.

5.
I was engaged to a Christian—
Tausk wrote in a split
case of a case study—
unwilling to convert,
and so was obliged to adopt
her faith to marry. Our sons
by this marriage were baptized.
In due course we told them
about their background, lest
they be swayed by views
at school. Once at a summer
house of a teacher, in D.,
while we were sitting at tea
with our friendly hosts—
who hadn't an inkling of
our ancestry—the teacher's wife
took up a pointed attack
on the Jews. Afraid of the awkward
exchange that would no doubt ensue,
and alarmed at the prospect of ruining
our trip, and losing our lodgings,
I held my tongue, and listened.
But fearing my sons in their candid
way would soon betray
the truth, I tried to send them
out of the room, but slipped,
and instead of saying "Go
into the garden *Jungen*
(young ones)," I said *Juden*
(Jews). The courage, it seems,
of my convictions had broken
through. And the subterranean,
faith of our fathers, I found,
could not simply be

dismissed as chance, since one
is always another's heir
and might in time become
a harbinger of one's own.

———

New façades and prim homes
show us no more than color and form,
not what's living, lurking, within.
Concealed things, Tausk told Lou
(1912, mid-December,
as the two were drawing closer),
are best revealed by those Jews
used to viewing ancient rooms
through the scrim of crumbling ruins.

———

I don't know if you are right
(Freud to one Enrico Morselli)
in your judgment which wants to see
psychoanalysis as an explicit
product of the Jewish spirit;
but if that's what it turned out to be,
I wouldn't feel ashamed of it.

o

We held within us dark forces
(Freud said of a friend he'd miss)
inaccessible to analysis—
that something which is most mysterious
and makes the Jew just what he is.

6.
We do live through more than we are, wrote Lou.
Or are we more than we normally live through?

————

How nicely Tausk put it last night:
    Commonplaceness comes, he noted,
       not from lack of spirit only
         but far more from a lack of life.

All of living's affirmation
    is rooted in great depth of feeling—
       through what *can't* quite be controlled
        in linkage's limitless intimation.

————

… So the lover flees the lonesome
agon into another's extension,
confusing, said Tausk, dying and pleasure's
blessed eclipse of the sense that *I am* …

————

Freud acts with complete conviction
    proceeding sharply against Tausk.
Along with the analyst's fact
    (of Tausk's neurotic disposition),
it's also clear that independence
    around Freud—marked by displays

of temper and tantrums, or aggression—
   worries and wounds him automatically
in his explorer's noble egoism,
   forcing premature discussion,
inevitably. Rank, who's always a son
   and nothing but (and whose tuition
Freud arranged for, as with Tausk's),
   is far more to be desired.
Why, asks Freud, referring to his
   Viennese circle of disciples,
can't there be six of him and not just one?

———

Freud on Tausk, to Lou one night
after the break with Jung, his "son,"
on why, for now, Tausk was the right
man to have at hand: "He's clever
and dangerous. He can bark *and* bite."

———

Only now do I perceive
the whole tragedy of Tausk's situation,
Lou suddenly sees in her journal—
1913, late summer:
He'll always take on the same problems
and tackle the same lines of attack
Freud takes up, never creating
room for himself. It isn't chance.
It indicates his making of self
a son as violently as he hates

the father for this configuration.
What he wants is blind and dumb
self-expression. Suffering so
under the burden of his own person.
And this as well: Perhaps a certain
hole in creativity is filled
through that murky identification
with the father (as the son),
which in time yields the illusion
that he's achieved the exalted fusion.

———

I. M.——an Influence
    Machine, in short;
and we are what we
    become in its import.

o

The Invention of Influence?
    I can hear the sigh
as it's reduced to
    the I of I.

———

Curious, too, how he can come
upon the most profound discoveries
in analyses——displacements all,
    of his desire to be discovered
    by another *through* analysis——

missing things directly before him
when they're pitched over *his* abyss.

———

Then she spoke of maternal being—
his, although it wasn't in him—
between the beast of his daily prey
and his precious self-dissolution.
It's all so painful to see, she said,
that one would rather look away,
or flee. It's himself he's deceiving
with his fantasies. Something wraithlike
and impure resonates through him, buzzing,
as though with murmurings from within.
And yet, from the very beginning
she understood that it was true—
it was the struggle in him that moved her,
"that of the Brother-Animal—You."

PART THREE

"I am allowing this horsecart of fate
to run across me," he wrote from Lublin
as chief physician at the wards,
where, in September, he was stationed.

"We shall see with what a skeleton
I'll start a new life after the war."
Thus Tausk to his ex-wife,
living in Zagreb with his mother

because she'd run out of money and sent
the boys away to school as boarders
until their troubles might subside.
1916, six months later,

his father died: "Peace to this
much-tested man," he wired home,
as though he were writing his own eulogy.
He began writing of war symptomology—

peasant conscripts who took on the look
of sad and sick domestic animals,
others wound with convulsive tics,
adrift, as he put it, in "twilight states";

a depressed paranoiac calls out—"Sir,
I wish to report that I am a deer,"
having been shot like a buck as he leapt
from tree to tree, fear to fear.

He tried to spare men execution
for turning their backs to rubrics of duty
defined in terms they'd never known—
patients bound by law to join

"in the destruction of human beings
and human value, people shipped
like ammunition to their ruin.
I began this work with the greatest aversion,

having escaped sitting in judgment
of others when I was younger and served
before and over the courts of the Law;
but now I must account for myself

with this insight whose worth is greater
to my country in the end
than the death of a few malingerers.
Forgive me," offered the difficult doctor—

a charismatic and chronic deserter
of others, said some, and his own nature,
"for shielding a boy who would not slaughter
a shackled group of enemy prisoners

or one overcome as if by forces
from without—though speaking through him;
and restless wandering fugitive souls
in petty flight from paternal compulsion,

or frightened flight from impending madness,
or noble flight to a flimsy ideal—
driven by sickness-for-home run amok,
swirling like eidolons of the real;

however decrepit and wretched they are,
fleeing while betters are being condemned—
without pity, to manure the soil
with their flesh and with their blood—

these too merit the mercy
of a Law that looks within the son
and sees the wound the father inflicted
causing infantilized soldiers to run—

men no worse than many others . . ."
(Tausk closed his "serious survey,
with serious words spoken in jest")
". . . who also evade the general suffering

and cannot renounce their gratification,
and fill their heart's desire like children,
and whom the term deserter would honor—
because they live on *profit* from war."

o

He acted, wrote Freud, in his obituary,
heroically—throwing himself wholeheartedly
into exposing the many abuses
that doctors committed or feebly excused.

2.

4 December
        1918,
again in Vienna,
        again to Martha—
"It flutters in
        my head," he said,
promising to
        send more soon
and noting that he
        hadn't yet
earned a thing.
        "The patients Freud
refers don't come.
        … And no one
wants to spend
        money—they
need it all
        for food. The other
doctors, too,
        have nothing to do."

———

A few weeks later,
Freud refused him
   analysis with
the father he'd master
   within the disaster
he'd always almost
   just become
(his trouble with love
   in particular
being what he'd

hoped to discuss).
"A dog on a leash"
    is what Tausk was,
he told a colleague
from their circle,
    "he'll eat me up";
instead he referred him
    to a disciple,
his analysand—
the bridge between them
    a woman again.

For twelve weeks
the two considered
Tausk's response
    to the refusal:
his grieving sense
    of dismissal at heart,
and paranoid notions
his thoughts were being
    somehow sifted
by the Master
(whose thinking he was).
    And still his self-
sufficiency drew him,
always that distant
    presence within.
His analyst's sessions
    with Freud, in turn,
were given almost
    wholly over
to what Tausk told her
    during their hour.

Then they were done.

———

Whoever possesses my *mysterion*,
   a rabbi recorded, is my son.

o

The hand extending toward the victim,
   said another, gives birth to him.

o

Let the honor of your disciple,
   said the son of one of the fathers,
   be like that of your own name;
and that of your name like fear of your teacher;
and fear of your teacher like his of shame.

o

Eliezer once defied the majority
   and God on high took his side,
sending His voice down from heaven.
The rabbis, however, quoted the Deity
   to himself, Deuteronomy 30:
   It (the teaching) isn't in heaven!
And the Lord laughed with joy and replied:
My sons, he cried, have defeated me!

———

Tausk's task
    was simple enough:
become the aggressor
    by being crushed,
and be a good son
    by committing the sin
of dying to show
    what the master was missing.

———

He liked to liken his students to dogs
taking a bone from the table to chew it
    in a corner, on their own.
    But, he'd note, it is *my* bone.

———

March 26, to Lou once again
in Göttingen:

"Freud shows respect,
    but little warmth.
Nevertheless,
our relations are better
    now that I
seek them no longer.

Much better
they cannot become.

But I've at last
been cured
        of my
    desire for them."

3.
"Lieber Herr Professor," he writes
to his teacher three months later,
assuming a casual form of address
and asking the master to please excuse
his absence from the evening lecture.
"I," Tausk announced, "am occupied
with the decisive affairs of my life
and do not want by contact with you
to be tempted to seek your assistance."
The tone was odd, the language awkward—
Tausk's—but somehow altered. "I hope
to soon be free," he adds, "to approach you,"
noting that he planned "to appear
with a minimum of neurosis."

———

Later that night,
        the early hours:

Lieber Herr Professor,
Please render assistance to my
        beloved fiancée, Miss Hilda
Loewi (II Kornergasse 2),
        the dearest woman who ever came
into my life. She will not ask
        much of you. I thank you for all
the good you have done me. It was much—
        and has given meaning to these
last ten years of my life.
        Your work is genuine, and great. I depart

this world knowing that I was among
   those who witnessed the triumph of one
of the greatest ideas of humankind.
   I have no melancholy. My suicide is
the healthiest and most decent deed
   of my derailed existence. My heart
holds no resentment. I accuse
no one of anything. I'm only dying
   somewhat earlier than I might have
died naturally. . . .
         I greet you warmly—
            Yours,
               Tausk

Please, also look after my sons
from time to time.

                    ——

"I am taking leave of my life
which I have undermined methodically
and worked to degrade since I was young,
and which has now completely lost"—
he wrote in his last will and testament,
3 July, one thirty,
while he was sipping plum brandy—
"its meaning, since I cannot any
longer enjoy it. My talent is,"
he concluded, "too meager to
sustain me. The recognition that I
cannot enter a new marriage,
can only keep myself and my

beloved fiancée in torment,
constitutes the true, conscious
motive of my suicide. Goodbye—
mother, brothers, sisters, and friends.
Live better than I did, dear sons.
Forget me, as soon as you can . . .
I have deceived you all by living
a role to which I was not equal."

4.
Then he was gone,
gone but there,
    a corpse in the air;
a crater punched
    in his head by his gun,
he hanged from a cord
as a carcass is hung.
Now he was no one—
"the father of im-
    purity's fathers"
is what the fathers
called a cadaver;
    and yet, at last
(within the chain
    of his tradition)
Tausk had become
    more than he'd been
and spurned all along.
Peace to this man,
    this much-tested son.
Now he was one
who'd speak from beyond.

                    o

I want to tell you
                how (he'd written)
it ends (years
                earlier): *your heaven
becoming ever*
                more narrow,
and all distances
                *departing toward you
daily from the*
                horizon, to crush you …

5.

1 August   Dear Frau Andreas
        (Freud writes), Poor Tausk,
        whom you favored with your friendship
        for some time, took his life
        on 3.7. He had returned
        worn out from the horrors of war
        and was intending to remarry,
        but reconsidered (so F. put it).
        What was behind it we cannot guess.
        He spent his days wrestling with
        the father-ghost. I confess,
        I do not really miss him. I've known
        for quite some time that he was useless—
        and, indeed, a future threat.

            Once or twice I had the occasion
        to glance at the foundations on which
        his high-flown sublimations rested . . .
        and long ago would have dropped him,
        if *you* had not raised him so
        in my estimation. . . .

            For my old age I have chosen
        the theme of death. I've stumbled on
        a most remarkable notion, rooted
        in my theory of the instincts,
        and now must read all sorts of things
        new to me but pertinent to it.
        I am not fond, however, of reading.
        With warmest greetings,
                        Yours,
                            Freud

6.

That a son can't bear his name is a shame, or a sham,
like one who's not quite his own man
(a sun with a "u"—to a larger system).
A son with an "O" of address, or an "o"—as before
the "h"—of a sigh, says I am only I in relation.
And yet, sons make a nation.

Sons for some are angels,
for others baubles, or squinting infants,
a kind of endorsement,
or not what was meant. Or a torment.
A grown son referred to as such, it's true,
is often a kind of embarrassment.

One son is said to be God, or God's.
Another's merely a mother's deity.
A son is a link in a chain that links, like a gang's,
or a tutelary. Being a son involves a bond
or being bound. It's a tie that blinds and defines.
That keeps one in line. At times it's like wine,

but then it's a chink in the good old armor.
The favorite son is often a charmer.
A son might marry the farmer's daughter
and have sons or a son's daughters.
Certain sons are marked for slaughter.
Once a son, always a son, even when one is a father.

But sometimes a son is a *door* to the father.
And then that son's seeing is double,
and so he believes that relation is noble

and the sole source of becoming singular
so as to matter, somehow, to others.
Thus a son gives birth to his brothers.

That a son is a name, then, isn't a game,
though it is up for grabs. And that's not a shame,
it's a tradition. A son's an emission.
Desire's expression. A bearer of cues, and clues,
a spooked thing—and maybe an influence, or just a fluency,
demanding or dormant, through you, through me.

CODA

It is, said the doctor, a machine
    of a mystical nature—
depicted in detail by certain patients.
    Their confidence notwithstanding,
these witnesses are able to offer
    only the vaguest of hints
as to *how* this heirloom functions.
    It makes them see pictures. It produces
thoughts and feelings, and also removes them,
    by means of curious forces.
It triggers disruptions within the body—
    visions and even effusion,
a tangible kind of impregnation,
    as one becomes a host.
For some it's driven by faint effluvia
    derived from human breath
or death; for others suggestions are sent
    on waves into the brain.
It's born of a need to explain the cause
    of things inherent in man.
Various elements are always involved:
    Enemies. Displaced erotic
tension. Boundaries are called into question,
    as though one's thoughts were "given"
and understanding received from beyond.
    Knowing is never owned.
One is next to nothing alone.
    Strings are pulled and buttons
pressed, all to elude an anxiety
    that rears its head at the heart

of the void in avoidance. The echoes start:
   The cure's an illness, the illness
a cure. Thus the revolving door
   that becomes a lament for the makers—
and for those who fall prey to the powers—
   of this most intricate machine.

III

A BYZANTINE DIPTYCH

I. LEVITICUS AGAIN

And his issue is unclean, 15:3

He is human and so will be humbled
He is flesh and so will fail
He is bone and so will be broken
He is blood and so will bleed
He has cheated and so will be changed
He has deceived and so will be drained
He has mocked and so will be muddied
He is hollow and so will howl
He has sullied and so will sadden
He is nothing and so will be nought
He is pain and so will perish
He is emission and so will be missed
He is water and so will weep
He is cavernous and so will cry
He is dross and so will disgust
He is a carcass and so will be cast
He has soured and so will stink
He is rank and so will retch
He is a worm and so will writhe
He is corruption and will be betrayed
He came forth, and so he will fade

II. ON WHAT IS NOT CONSUMED

And the angel of the Lord was revealed to him

[in the heart of the flame]

Exodus 3:2

Angel of fire devouring fire
Fire Blazing through damp and drier
Fire Candescent in smoke and snow
Fire Drawn like a crouching lion
Fire Evolving through shade after shade
Fateful fire that will not expire
Gleaming fire that wanders far
Hissing fire that sends up sparks
Fire Infusing a swirling gale
Fire that Jolts to life without fuel
Fire that's Kindled and kindles daily
Lambent fire unfanned by fire
Miraculous fire flashing through fronds
Notions of fire like lightning on high
Omens of fire in the chariots' wind
[Pillars of fire in thunder and storm]
[Quarries of] fire wrapped in a fog
Raging fire that reaches Sheol
T[errible fire that Ushers in] cold
Fire's Vortex like a Wilderness crow
Fire eXtending and Yet like a rainbow's
Zone of color arching through sky

Yannai, Palestine, c. 6ᵗʰ century C.E.

ABULAFIA SAID THAT

the letters of the name of God
　　add up in Hebrew to eighty-six,
as do those of the word Nature.
Such is the nature of his nature's tricks.

THE PERFECT STATE

1.

The perfect state of being human isn't perfection,
it's becoming, the Greeks say, ever more real
in nearing but never quite reaching a certain ideal,
like translation. It's deficient. A chronic affection.

2.

Perfection for the Kabbalist is reached
only when the fortress is breached
to the brokenness, the husks, the Other Side.
So imperfection becomes a guide.

3.

Ancient aspirants imagined perfection
as progress up—to palaces on high.
For us the question is can one bring
that heightened vision into an eye?

4.

Perfection doesn't entail a return
to a wholeness where one never yearns,
as female is fused to male, back-to-back.
Perfection's in facing what we lack.

5.
Perfection, the feeling philosopher says,
suggests an openness to endless change—
the self in radical revolution
within a self it soon finds strange.

6.
The spirit warrior's path to perfection
comprises trials involving great fear—
an allegorical learning to fathom
the power passing through one's ear.

7.
The mind's movement toward perfection
is joy, said the Jew who continued to grind
the glass that would kill him—and sorrow is in
our knowing we're leaving perfection behind.

8.
A person approaches her perfect nature,
and becomes herself in the truest sense,
by acceding at times to the angel within her—
its flitting presence her only defense

against perfection's petrifaction,
suggests Avicenna's *Celestial Ascent*
(pun intended), as subtraction
leads her to more than she ever meant.

NOTES FROM AN ESSAY ON THE UNCANNY

for Kenneth Gross

1.

The puppets guide our souls through The Dance.
Strange how jerks can hold us in a trance.

2.

Bizarre—a dead-thing yielding the thrill
of feeling through fear a lifeline's pull.

3.

The puppet's secret infuses the air,
although its master's hand is seen there.

4.

He's one with its syntax, again in a mask,
driven by the pulse of another's poem—
odd how this being afloat in the foreign
is the closest he'll come to being at home.

5.

Is that a broken doll in the ruin,
or a votive offering—to the moon?

6.
They're all surface, shadows on a screen,
degrees of darkness revealed between
their maker and those who watch them fade—
when their tale's told—into the unmade.

7.
Abstracted from matter cut with a knife,
they channel that frangible power: life.

8.
Their images mounted on a spinning wheel
engender shadows that are somehow more real
than the source making them flit there before us
across that screen, a curious chorus.

So flickering figments replace their brothers,
and this generation follows the others.

THE QUALMIST AGING

I lift my eyes to my pills,
whence cometh my help.

·

OKAY, KOUFONISSI

on one of the Little Cyclades

1

Okay, Koufonissi, our island, we're back
in your silk-robe quiet, and water, and wind.

2

Not bad, Koufonissi, *you're* back
in our faces with your softness.

3

Alright, Koufonissi, we've spent the night
with your stillness, your heat, your tedium.

4

Your sea, Koufonissi, like turquoise crayons
from the box with violets and darker blues.

5

Scorpena, sand-smelt, bogue, and bream
swim within Koufonissi's dream.

6

Keros, island-door to the world below,
silent across the bay from this heaven.

7

Taxí isn't a taxi in Greek, it just means "okay."
There are no taxis on Koufonissi, but all is well.

8

The island throughout which nothing is heard.
Only the wind in the shell of the word.

9

A birthmark in the Aegean
is all you are, Koufonissi.

10

Night after night and the boats putter out,
then hover—spirits over the water.

11

What's with those smashed figurines, O Keros—
Cycladic anger four thousand years old?

12

What dreams, Koufonissi, you prompt—
nightmares in Atlantis. How strange.

13

Orion is plugged, Koufonissi,
into your blackening moonless sky.

14
It's true, Koufonissi, this idyll
isn't life—it's vacation. And yet . . .

15
Ah, Koufonissi, the mysteries
of getting those schools into your nets.

SUMMER SYNTAX

Saxifrage, arabis, phlox;
lobelia, euphorbia, nasturtium;
coreopsis, guara, flax;
brunnera, salvia, rubrum;

delphinium, snapdragon, alyssum;
bacopa, yarrow, thyme;
viola, cress, chrysanthemum,
convolvulus and clematis that climb

over the flowering fescue,
the prairie mallow, and sage,
with Lucerne sisyrinchium to the rescue
of spirit surveying the cage

of its inching calibrations—
luring us out to stare
into this constellation's
efflorescence as   everywhere.

QUATRAINS FOR A CALLING

Why are you here?
Who have you come for
and what would you gain?
Where is your fear?

Why are you *here*?

You've come so near,
or so it would seem;
you can see the grain
in the paper—that's clear.

But why are you here

when you could be elsewhere,
earning a living
or actually learning?
Why should we care

why you're here?

Is that a tear?
Yes, there's pressure
behind the eyes—
and there are peers.

But why are *you* here?

At times it sears.
The pressure and shame
and the echoing pain.
What do you hear

now that you're here?

The air's so severe.
It calls for equipment,
which comes at a price.
And you've volunteered.

Why? Are you here?

What will you wear?
What will you do
if it turns out you've failed?
How will you fare?

Why are you here

when it could take years
to find out—what?
It's all so slippery
and may not cohere.

And yet, you're here . . .

Is it what you revere?
How deep does that go?
How do you know?
Do you think you're a seer?

Is *that* why you're here?

Do you have a good ear?
For praise or for verse?
Can you handle a curse?
Define persevere.

Why *are* you here?

It could be a career.

SELF-PORTRAIT IN PIECES

1. REJECTED COMMISSION

I've always wanted to publish a self-
portrait, and this, in fact, just may be it,
or at least a start. There's more soon to come.
There's always more. Above all once it's done.

2. DEFLECTED COMMISSION

"You must learn," the Japanese teacher of drawing
said to the foreign student who, it seems, was drawn
toward the impressionistic, "to respect reality."
Precisely. And so, I write what's just beyond me.

3. SELF-PORTRAIT IN A 14TH-CENTURY MIRROR
(again after Santob)

I keep myself young and lithe
but not because I'm afraid of age—
    I'm afraid of people
who'd see me and think I was wise.

SIX CHEERS FOR VON HOFMANNSTHAL

1.

He, in being himself, was funneling
the other selves in time he'd release,
a music of ten thousand voices
flowing into the frames he'd see
fit to arrange through the years of his choices—
the ideal more real than the actual then.

2.

His universe shattered, shard into shard.
Words began to float like eyes,
gazing at him and making it hard
not to stare into their swirl
which swept him toward the rim of the void.

3.

Through what's without he saw within.

He saw not a thing within without
the world that was always a thought beyond

until he emerged from his redoubt.

4.

Plasticity yields a dignity.
And yet a person needs to wield
a certain transcendental vanity.

5.
Depth, above all, he sought to conceal
along the surface his weave would reveal.

6.
Man, he wrote, is manifold.

MORE ON FINISHING

But is the incompleteness of knowing
the open-endedness of its flowing—

which art that's worth even part of its weight
in materials learns to demonstrate?

Or is insistence on process the mark
of a dilettante's groping in the dark?

PHILO IN HIS CONFUSION

Philo in his *Confusion of Tongues*
broods on things that are often blurred:
We're not quite sons, he cautions, of God—
but might be children of the Word.

TUTELARY

Solace from anemones,
sepals of instinct pushing the air.
Why do they matter so much, there
in the room at noon while nothing moves
around them: scarlet, creams, and burgundies,
magenta, bone-white, and bruise-like blues;
the wind's daughter, or bride, for some,
for others a temple to the wounds of Tammuz—
or living itself, wordless, longing.
Where *is* that luminous lusciousness from?

A SONG OF DISSENT

In the Kingdom of knowing
what we've known,
at speech's Foundation
where no one's just one,
even as Majesty's
magic links us,
the stink of Eternity's
purity numbs.
The spirit sinking
in abstract Splendor
longs for the tactile
aspect of Power,
so harshness becomes
Grace's facet—
Insight's angle
onto the fog—
and the start of Wisdom
is a misty dictum,
the Crown of it nothing
but the fear of some God.

ON MAKING AND BEING MADE

Onto your waters, craft,
I cast my muse's raft—

as ... into your hands, *technē,*
I commend the day's debris.

PATHETIC

It seemed sick, really, or pathetic:
fertilizer bombs being wired in Gaza,
    flesh scraped from a Tel Aviv bus;
    radar whirring miles above us,
state-sanctioned torture up the street,
and information like an epidemic—

but I took some comfort today, for hours,
from a kitten we found near a mound of garbage
    and nursed back from the edge of death.
    By evening, I could feel its breath
against the skin of my neck as it slept—
and reconfigured my notions of power.

WHAT MAKES OUR SENSE MAKE SENSE

What babble is it that languages echo?
What echoes percolate there in its midst
indistinctly, but nonetheless
through syntax—
                    in its seasoned reasoning?
What prattle is it that makes our sense
make sense? What voiceless glyph masks
its start with absence? What premise is this?

The vapor of the Preacher's vanity?
Breath whispered through speech's reed?
And why would anyone need to know
it's a sign that brings within reach
miraculous aspects of an instinct
that has us asking *How are things?*
and hearing—
                    behind each answer's door
something drawing us through confusion
and toward a wordless core that sings?

BEING LED

As I write I'm being led
by matter older than I am
(but from the place where I was born)—
a yellow pencil on which the words
Again the Leader—
                    1946 Chevrolet,
Paterson, N.J.
have been engraved.

The eraser, however, is less
than useless
(using it only makes matters worse
and blurs what appears on the page).

It surfaced somehow not long ago:

I found it among my father's papers.

The pleasure it affords is strange.

WHAT IS

for MRM, in memoriam

The Norway maple's chartreuse crown
in April ciphers autumn's flares,
startling with mace-like spikelets of flowers
swelling over the paths of that square

where we wander, adrift in the branching—
or is it what's branching adrift in us—
wafted as if afloat on a wisdom
flowing through this city forest.

The grid encodes an understanding:
Those who stroll past tines of elms,
who'll wade the shade of summer's linden
and trace the mottled bark of planes,

move as though of their own accord
but under invisible gates of a grace
born in their being borne along
or gradually dying to the spell of the place

where dogs are walked and judgment is rendered
and power, as weakness, brings down limbs;
where mercy's continual averment is tendered,
and children at recess dart into rings;

where a woman's will surges through her
sitting alone in the rinse of her cancer,
as the vapor of chatter's released to the air.
All part of the terrible splendor—

the weeping cherry shedding petals,
like snow in an ancient ocular rhyme—
the sight, of course, is a site of convention,
the tiniest of triumphs over time,

and yet—somehow, the sarabande combines
as majesty. The rupture and gentle carriage
of kindness. The wind's extended winding
kiss. The almost now actual: a marriage

not so much of opposites as,
say, analogous aspects—exits
to entrances, or attics holding an axial
weave of sound's foundation. The praxis

perfecting opens into. An instant's
happiness putting us back in the business
of funneling the whole shebang, which Kabbalists
have given a name. Kingdom. What is.

NOTES

EPIGRAPH: Hugo Rennert was a German engineer and amateur painter who was committed to an asylum in 1902. He was pursued by voices and felt himself to be penetrated by X-rays that revealed his most intimate secrets and desires. Rennert's vivid account of his condition, from which the epigraph is taken, was written as a kind of self-diagnosis while he was institutionalized. From *Air Loom: The Air Loom and Other Dangerous Influencing Machines*, edited by Thomas Röske and Bettina Brand-Claussen (Prinzhorn Collection, 2006), p. 122.

ACTUAL ANGELS: Epigraph: Rashi's commentary is to Genesis 32:4, where Jacob sends *malakhim* to Esau in Edom. The primary meaning of *malakhim* in biblical Hebrew is "messengers," but it can also mean "messengers of God," i.e., angels. (7) Angels abound in Jewish texts, and these four are explicitly mentioned as exalted forces in the Merkavah tradition, or the mystical "literature of the Chariot." (8) Abulafia throughout this collection is the Kabbalist Avraham Abulafia (1240–c. 1292), who was born in Spain and wandered for much of his adult life throughout the Mediterranean. His writing often deals with a transformative and visionary manipulation of language. See *The Poetry of Kabbalah: Mystical Verse from the Jewish Tradition*, translated and annotated by Peter Cole (Yale, 2012), pp. 108ff. (9) Paul Klee's "Angelus Novus," which Walter Benjamin writes about as the angel of history. (18) In the Jewish and Christian apocalyptic literature of Late Antiquity, Enoch is the seventh descendant of Adam and Eve: "Enoch walked with God. Then he was no more, for God took him" (Genesis 5:24). In the various books that emerge from this tradition, Enoch became Metatron, the most powerful of angels, who saw the secrets of creation's mystery. (19) Psalms 104:4, more commonly rendered as "He makes the winds his messenger."

ON FINISHING: "The sober Saba" is Umberto Saba, the Italian poet (1883–1957).

MORE FOR SANTOB: Santob de Carrión was a fourteenth-century Hebrew and Spanish poet. The group of poems gathered here, adapted from his Spanish collection, *Proverbios Morales*, builds on the much longer "Suite for Santob," which appears in *Hymns & Qualms* (Sheep Meadow, 1998, reissued in *What Is Doubled: Poems 1981–1998*, Shearsman Books).

SONG OF THE SHATTERING VESSELS: According to sixteenth-century Kabbalistic mythology, in order for God to create the universe, He first had to open a void within Himself to make room for creation. He then sent light through that void into vessels He'd prepared to channel the divine emanation. The light proved too powerful, however, and some of the vessels shattered—scattering sparks of divine light throughout the cosmos. As Kabbalists see it, the task of men and women is to gather up those sparks from the world of matter in what Gershom Scholem calls a continual "process of cosmic . . . reintegration." This dynamic of contraction and expression, rupture and restoration describes not only God's primordial creation, but all acts of ongoing creation.

Also central to the concern of this poem is the likening of speech to a kiss, and the role of the letters of the alphabet in the construction of the world. Abulafia's teacher, Barukh Togarmi, notes in his commentary to *Sefer Yetzirah* (the Book of Creation): "And it is said: twenty-two letters . . . are the foundation of the entire world, and this is the secret of, 'Mouth to mouth I will speak to him,' that is, in the union of the king and the queen, that is, in the kiss" (Moshe Idel, *The Mystical Experience in Abraham Abulafia* [SUNY, 1988], p. 184).

THE RELUCTANT KABBALIST'S SONNET: "Desire" and "the essence of speech" have identical numerological values in Hebrew— 417 (Elliot R. Wolfson, *Language, Eros, Being* [Fordham, 2005], p. 317). Gematria, or Hebrew numerology, played a central part in the mystical calculus of many Kabbalists, highlighting suprarational links between modes of experience and being. It was especially prominent in the work of Abulafia. The epigraph also recalls Adam Phillips's writing that "words, according to Freud, are what we do our wanting with."

THE INVENTION OF INFLUENCE: Victor Tausk (1879–1919) was one of Freud's most gifted early disciples in Vienna. He is best known for a paper he wrote in the final year of his life, "On the Origin of the 'Influencing Machine' in Schizophrenia."

The passages in italics in Part One are radically reworked excerpts from translations of Tausk's poetry. He prepared his poems for publication in 1915, but they were never printed in book form during his lifetime; a volume of his literary and psychoanalytic works was published in German in 1983 (*Gesammelte psychoanalytische und literarische Schriften*, edited by Hans-Joachim Metzger, Medusa). For help with the German, deep thanks are due to Ela Naegele. Other information in the poem is drawn from the following sources: Tausk's papers on psychoanalytic topics, which are now collected in English translation as *Sexuality, War and Schizophrenia* (edited by Paul Roazen, translated by E. Mosbacher et al, Transaction Publishers, 1991); *Minutes of the Vienna Psychoanalytic Society, 1906–1918* edited by H. Nunberg and E. Federn (International Universities Press, 1962); *The Freud Journal of Lou Andreas-Salomé*, translated by Stanley A. Levy (Basic Books, 1964) and *Sigmund Freud and Lou Andreas-Salomé: Letters*, edited by Ernst Pfeiffer, translated by W. and E. Robson-Scott (Norton, 1985); Freud's obituary for Tausk, which appears in the Hogarth Press *Standard Edition* of his work, edited by J. Strachey (vol. 17, pp. 273–75); letters, journal entries, and essays by Tausk and also by his son, Marius. Much of this material, and the affair as a whole, was retrieved from oblivion by Paul Roazen's groundbreaking and controversial study of Tausk's relationship to Freud, *Brother Animal:*

The Story of Freud and Tausk (Knopf, 1969). Roazen lays bare what he called Tausk's "struggle" with Freud, which sheds complicated light on the master-disciple connection. Roazen believes that Tausk's suicide was deliberately suppressed in psychoanalytic circles. Roazen's book was answered with two furiously detailed volumes by K. R. Eissler, the founder and long-time director of the Freud archives—*Talent and Genius: A Psychoanalytic Reply to a Defamation of Freud* (Grove, 1971) and *Victor Tausk's Suicide* (International Universities Press, 1983). Articles by Mark Kanzer, Paul Neumarkt, and others were also consulted.

The Rabbinic passages in Part One (for the most part in quotation marks) are drawn from the mishnaic tractate generally known in English as *The Sayings of the Fathers* (Pirkei Avot). These sections often enfold traditional commentary to that tractate as well.

The Talmudic passage in Part Two ("The great Talmudic sage Eliezer") comes, in part, from *The Fathers According to Rabbi Nathan,* chapter 6 and *Sukkah* 28a. "My *mysterion*" in Part Three is from Pesikta Rabbati, chapter 5 (Moshe Idel, *Ben: Sonship and Jewish Mysticism* [Continuum, 2007], p. 187).

"Let the honor of your disciples" is based on *The Sayings of the Fathers* 4:15 and *The Fathers According to Rabbi Nathan* 27.

The story of Eliezer's defying the majority and being defeated (with God) by the other rabbis is from the Talmud, *Bava Metzi'a* 58a–59b.

"The father of impurity's fathers" is the ultimate degree of uncleanness according to Jewish law. See Rashi's commentary to Numbers 19:22 and *Pesachim* 1:6.

A BYZANTINE DIPTYCH: Yannai is one of the great Hebrew poets of Late Antiquity. His work was lost for the better part of a millennium and rediscovered only in the twentieth century. He lived in Palestine.

ABULAFIA SAID THAT: Scholar Moshe Idel suggests that Spinoza's identification of Nature and God derives from Abulafia's numerological observation. Zev Harvey, "Idel on Spinoza," *Journal for the Study of Religions and Ideologies* (Winter 2007), pp. 88–94.

THE PERFECT STATE: (4) The Jewish myth of the back-to-back androgyne can be found in numerous places, including the Talmud (*Erubin* 18a), the midrashic literature (*Genesis Rabbah* 55 and *Leviticus Rabbah* 14:1), and the *Zohar* (1:49a).

NOTES FROM AN ESSAY ON THE UNCANNY: Inspired by Kenneth Gross's *Puppet: An Essay on Uncanny Life* (University of Chicago, 2011).

OKAY, KOUFONISSI: Koufonissi is a tiny island near Naxos. Its name derives from the Greek for "deaf." Keros Island, across the bay from it, is now uninhabited but served as the site of a religious shrine during the Early Bronze Age. Mysterious ruins of smashed, flat-faced Cycladic marble figurines have been found there.

SIX CHEERS FOR VON HOFMANNSTHAL: Hugo von Hofmannsthal (1874–1929) gave up a highly promising career as a Stefan George–like lyric poet after an aesthetic/spiritual crisis, which he captures in the fictional "Letter of Lord Chandos" (1902). After that he wrote more outward-looking prose, libretti, and drama.

PHILO IN HIS CONFUSION: *On the Confusion of Tongues* is a work by Philo (born c. 20 B.C.E., Alexandria) consisting of his commentary to Genesis 11:1–9 and the Tower of Babel story.

A SONG OF DISSENT: The words in capital letters are the ten Kabbalistic *sefirot*, in ascending order. The *sefirot* are expressions or even translations of divine influence into existence, refracted attributes that reflect human qualities and processes as well.

WHAT MAKES OUR SENSE MAKE SENSE: This poem was inspired by Daniel Heller-Roazen's *Echolalias* (Zone Books, 2008). Heller-Roazen's father, Paul, wrote *Brother Animal*, which figured prominently in the composition of "The Invention of Influence."

BEING LED: For my father, Murray Cole (born Cohen), 1923–2010. *His* father, Louis Cohen, worked for many years for a car dealership in Paterson, N.J.

WHAT IS: For María Rosa Menocal (1952–2012), friend, neighbor, and scholar extraordinaire of Andalusian culture. The poem descends stanza by stanza through the relational matrix of the Kabbalistic *sefirot*, which appear in their traditional order and stream beneath the thirteenth-century surface of the literature she loved.

Peter Cole's books of poetry include *What Is Doubled: Poems 1981–1998* and *Things on Which I've Stumbled*. He has translated *The Poetry of Kabbalah: Mystical Verse from the Jewish Tradition* and *The Dream of the Poem: Hebrew Poetry from Muslim and Christian Spain, 950–1492*, as well as the work of Aharon Shabtai, Taha Muhammad Ali, Yoel Hoffmann, and Avraham Ben Yitzhak, among others. He is also the author (with Adina Hoffman) of a volume of nonfiction, *Sacred Trash: The Lost and Found World of the Cairo Geniza*. Cole has received numerous honors for his work, including a Guggenheim Foundation fellowship, the National Jewish Book Award for Poetry, the PEN Translation Award for Poetry, the American Library Association's prize for the Jewish Book of the Year, and an Award in Literature from the American Academy of Arts and Letters. He was named a MacArthur Fellow in 2007.